WILLIAM MORRIS
PATTERN & DESIGN

WILLIAM MORRIS
PATTERN & DESIGN

INTRODUCTION BY
JENNY LISTER

CONTENTS

WILLIAM MORRIS: PATTERN REVOLUTIONARY

Jenny Lister

Portrait of William Morris, 1884. Frederick Hollyer. Platinum print, 15.1 × 10.6 cm (6 × 4 in). V&A: 7715-1938. Given by Eleanor M. Hollyer

Artist, designer, businessman, author, socialist, conservationist: of all the roles and activities he energetically pursued during his lifetime, William Morris (1834–1896) is perhaps now known most of all as the creator of beautiful repeating patterns based on English garden flowers. These designs are remarkable for their variety, despite Morris's recognizable style, as well as for their longevity: from *Trellis*, the first wallpaper, designed in 1862, through the block-printed and woven furnishing fabrics for curtains and upholstery of the 1870s and 1880s, such as *Strawberry Thief* or *Acanthus*, to his last collaborative projects of the 1890s. Faithfully reproduced or adapted and recoloured to suit twenty-first-century tastes, whether printed on a summer dress or practical kitchen blind, or used in the background of a period film, Morris's patterns are part of the fabric of everyday visual culture.

During his lifetime Morris was known just as much for his facility with words, as a poet. Lectures for design students and working men's groups communicated his strongly felt ideas about the role of art and design, also revealing the innate contradictions between his success as a designer, manufacturer and retailer and his belief in a fairer society, in which humanity could live in balance with the environment. Along with other artists, designers and writers associated with the Arts and Crafts Movement, Morris challenged industrial production and commercial expansion, promoting functional but simple decorative design that restored power to craftspeople and makers. For Morris, pattern applied with complete understanding of the possibilities of natural materials and handmade techniques had a moral, life-enhancing integrity and purpose, requiring 'beauty, imagination and order'[1] to 'give people pleasure in the things they must perforce *use* [and] to give people pleasure in the things they must perforce *make*'.[2]

The aim of this book is to highlight the Victoria and Albert Museum's collection of repeating patterns designed for reproduction on wallpapers and furnishing fabrics by Morris and close associates. Like the V&A, Morris's company was founded in the 1860s, and a mutually formative relationship was forged through Morris's many different interactions with the museum, such as his decorative scheme for the V&A's Green Dining Room of 1866, frequent visits to study historical textiles, and a collections-shaping role as an adviser to the museum authorities. After his death, his daughter May Morris (1862–1938) successfully campaigned for a permanent collection and displays to acknowledge her father's many contributions. In turn, curators and scholars have catalogued and researched Morris's art and design to provide multifaceted accounts of his work for contemporary audiences to explore and enjoy.

EARLY LIFE

Morris was born in 1834 into a prosperous middle-class family. His father, also named William, was a City broker, commuting daily into London from the family home in Walthamstow, while his mother, Emma Shelton, was descended from a wealthy family from Worcester. Morris was the eldest surviving son, the third of nine siblings. William Morris Senior's investments in copper, tin and arsenic mines in the west of England delivered a comfortable income, by 1840 enough to install the family in the substantial country estate of Woodford Hall in Essex and provide Morris with an inheritance that later allowed him to pursue a career in art and design. His childhood coincided with the expansion of the British Empire and the nation's transition into an industrialized society, with more than 50 per cent of the population living in cities by the 1851 census, when he was 16. Much of the landscape was transformed by the building of factories, railways and terraced houses – as well as new churches, often in the Gothic Revival style. In contrast to the lives of children of working-class families, Morris's early days in rural Essex were spent gardening, fishing, exploring parklands and country churches, or reading; he especially enjoyed the romantic adventure novels of Sir Walter Scott, which fuelled his interest in medieval history. Another favourite from the Woodford Hall library was *Gerard's Herball*, a sixteenth-century guide to botany, illustrated with woodcuts, a possible reference point for his later floral designs.

While his interest in textiles did not come into focus until adulthood, Morris did recall his first sight of historic tapestries of 'faded greenery' at a Tudor hunting lodge in Epping Forest.[3] This experience would inspire his 'bright dream', the revival of the craft of medieval tapestry making. After a few years away at boarding school, by 1851 Morris was studying for the Oxford entrance exams while living in the family home, now at Water House, Walthamstow, which later became the William Morris Gallery. This was the year of the Great Exhibition in Hyde Park, championing new manufactures. It was attended by over six million people, but Morris refused to visit; he had no wish to celebrate the excessively decorated and industrially produced products on display.[4]

OXFORD AND BLOOMSBURY

Planning a career as a clergyman, Morris studied theology at Oxford University. Student life provided him with the freedom to explore new interests and make life-changing friendships. With Edward Burne-Jones (1833–1898) and others he formed a 'brotherhood', focused on art, literature and history. Inspired by John Ruskin's 'The Nature of Gothic' (1853), Morris spent the summers touring medieval cathedrals in northern France. In 1856 he began an

apprenticeship with G.E. Street (1824–1881), leading architect of the Gothic Revival. Morris wrote to a friend of his new mission with typical exuberance: 'I MUST make haste, it would not do for me … to be a lazy, aimless, useless, dreaming body all my life long.'[5] Following the pioneering lead of A.W.N. Pugin (1812–1852), Street recommended the study of medieval textiles, particularly embroidery, and his new versions designed with stylized fruit and flowers became widely used in Victorian churches. Morris's exposure to ecclesiastical textiles during this time sparked his career as a designer and hands-on craftsman. His apprenticeship also brought him into contact with the architect Philip Webb (1831–1915), with whom a profoundly creative friendship grew from a shared love of vernacular buildings and many different craft disciplines.

With encouragement from Burne-Jones and the Pre-Raphaelite artist Dante Gabriel Rossetti (1828–1882), now a friend, Morris changed direction again. Determined to focus on fine art and painting, he contributed to an ambitious scheme decorating the Oxford Union debating hall with scenes from Arthurian legends. About this time he first encountered Jane Burden (1839–1914). The daughter of a stableman, and from a very different social background, she agreed to model for Rossetti and Morris. A painting by Morris gives us a glimpse into his rented London rooms, probably near to the time of his engagement to Jane: she is shown as Queen Iseult from the fifteenth-century romance *Le Morte d'Arthur*, while the interior is styled in imitation of an illumination for the *Froissart Chronicles* of 1470–74, with a Turkish rug, embroidered hangings and a table cover resembling an altar frontal [FIG. 1].

RED HOUSE

Morris and Jane Burden married in 1859. Red House, in Bexleyheath, Kent, the home they created together in collaboration with Webb and Burne-Jones, was radical in design and medieval in style, and exemplified the principles that were the foundation of the Arts and Crafts Movement. The brick-built structure referenced local architecture and materials, and every detail, inside and out, was imbued with references to literature, art or personal meaning. The Morrises and their friends created a vibrantly decorated home, a 'palace of art' celebrating favourite legends and medieval texts, particularly Chaucer's poem *The Legend of Good Women* (c.1385). They stencilled patterns on walls and ceilings, decorated furniture with delicate narrative paintings, and embroidered hangings that depicted human figures as well as the repeating motifs that were becoming part of the emerging 'Morrisian' style.

In the master bedroom, the decorated walls and furniture were complemented by embroideries worked in wool thread

on indigo-dyed wool by Jane Morris and her sister Bessie Burden (1841–1924) [FIG. 2]. Jane Morris recalled that her husband, delighted by some unfashionable plain blue cloth she had found in a London shop, 'set to work at once designing flowers – these we worked in bright colours in a simple rough way – the work went quickly'.[6] Clumps of similar daisies could be seen decorating stained-glass windows and painted tiles at Red House, as well as growing in the garden, which had been carefully planned as part of the whole concept. Set in an orchard, the garden extended to a meadow and an enclosed area divided with wooden trellis panels planted with climbing roses, jasmine and honeysuckle, sunflowers, marigolds, poppies and others, which would become familiar emblems in Morris's patterns.

'THE FIRM' AND MORRIS WALLPAPERS

In April 1861, seeing a potential market for their hand-crafted interiors for homes

FIG. 3 Design for *Trellis* wallpaper, November 1862. William Morris, birds drawn by Philip Webb. Pencil and watercolour, 66 × 61 cm (26 × 24⅛ in). William Morris Gallery, London Borough of Waltham Forest (BLA472)

and churches, Morris and seven of his friends launched the firm initially known as Morris, Marshall, Faulkner & Co. With the established names of Webb and Rossetti helping to secure commissions, the firm began to make a name for its decorating services. Jane Morris, Georgiana Burne-Jones (1840–1920), Kate Faulkner (1841–1898) and other talented women in the circle were always part of the enterprise, contributing their embroidery and painting skills as well as original designs. As the business expanded from the original workshops in Bloomsbury, central London, it became clear that Morris's hope to run the company from Red House was unsustainable. After only five years he sold the property and moved his young family – daughters Jenny and May were born in 1861 and 1862 – to live above the showroom at 26 Queen's Square in Bloomsbury.

The lower floors and ballroom of the large townhouse became a series of workshops and the operational base for the firm for the next 16 years. Among the first commercially produced products were wallpapers: *Trellis*, *Daisy* and *Fruit*, designs that recalled the gardens and interiors of Red House [FIG. 3]. On-site experiments proved ineffective, and production was contracted out to the long-established manufacturer Jeffrey & Co. As Emma Hardy's research has shown, these first three papers, hand block-printed with Morris's straightforward representations of garden flowers, enabled the firm to gain a foothold in the expanding market for wallpaper, helping to establish a broad base of customers, tapping into the increasing numbers of middle-class families in Britain's expanding cities with the disposable income to furnish their homes. The company was also commissioned to furnish the country homes of more artistically influenced businessmen and aristocrats. With the complementary embroidery designs, these wallpaper patterns helped build the brand, forming a clear visual identity for the firm that would stand the test of time.[7]

In the 1860s consumers were offered a bewildering range of novelty and choice in wallpaper and fabric patterns, which were mechanically produced on engraved metal rollers that facilitated fine detail and shading to create artificially colourful illusions of realistic flowers and lifelike scenes. Morris's first wallpapers implicitly responded to calls for reform, offering simple interpretations of nature that evoked real plant forms while acknowledging the flat walls they decorated. Other papers added to the range were based directly on historical sources, but from 1870 more characteristic patterns were introduced, such as *Lily*, *Powdered* and *Jasmine*. These had a more complex, layered structure, with a main large motif repeated against a background of small trailing leaves. Morris chose *Pimpernel*, a design dominated by overblown poppies encircled in their

FIG. 4 The dining room
at Kelmscott House,
Hammersmith, *c*.1896.
Photographed by Emery Walker.
Gelatin silver print, 29.5 ×
24.2 cm (11⅝ × 9⅝ in).
V&A: PH.1-1973

FIG. 5 Printing block
used for discharge printing
Kennet, designed in 1883,
probably carved by Alfred or
James Barrett. The Society
of Antiquaries of London,
Kelmscott Manor

stems but named after the flowers that compose the background pattern, to decorate the dining room at Kelmscott House, his London home from 1878. It provided a unifying backdrop for works of art including a Rossetti painting, a precious seventeenth-century Safavid carpet and a pair of brass peacocks from Iran [FIG. 4]. Morris's bedroom was much more simply decorated with *Trellis*, a constant reminder of the garden at Red House.[8]

PRINTING

Morris supervised the production and quality of the papers manufactured by Jeffrey & Co., developing a close working relationship with Metford Warner (1843–1930), the proprietor of the firm. The block-printing process began with the carving of the printing blocks, a specialist craft outsourced to the Barrett family, based in Bethnal Green. Surviving blocks are beautiful and informative objects in their own right, exhibiting the marks of the skilled wood-carving required [FIG. 5]. Pearwood was chosen for its very dense grain. The block cutter first copied the original design on the surface using tracing paper and, with Morris checking every stage, proceeded to cut separate blocks for every colour of the pattern, adding pins to leave registration dots for each impression.

Most papers were hand block-printed in distemper, a water-based paint made with ground chalk, size (glue) and pigment, which was transferred to the printing block from a pad soaked in the colour. The printing block was then placed on the paper and heavy pressure applied with a foot-operated lever. Once the whole length of paper was printed, the paper was left to dry before the next colour was added, if needed. For larger-scale and more complex patterns a great number of blocks were required: *Acanthus* was printed with 30 blocks, two for each colour,

   WILLIAM MORRIS: PATTERN REVOLUTIONARY

while the most expensive and prestigious paper made, for St James's Palace, required 68 in total. Retail prices varied accordingly, from five shillings a roll up to 30 shillings for a complex design such as *Chrysanthemum* when specified with an embossed finish or gold ground, or more for special orders.[9]

The printing of fabrics for curtains and soft furnishings essentially uses the same method, with the pigment or dye formulated as a thick paste and transferred to the cloth by the carved block and mallet [FIG. 6]. As for wallpapers, subtle variations and imperfections are inherent to the process and form a vital part of the appeal of the final product. By 1875 the wallpaper range, mostly designed by Morris himself, extended to about 17 patterns, which amounted to 67 different products in different colourways,

including some ceiling papers.[10] With Morris increasingly coordinating the firm's activities, it was reconstituted under his sole management as Morris & Co., entailing great responsibility but also creative freedom to explore his interest in textiles.

TEXTILES

For the following decade Morris focused on textile techniques and dyeing processes: hand block-printing, weaving, machine-woven and hand-knotted carpeting and ultimately tapestry weaving, seeking out like-minded specialists who could help him achieve the effects he desired in each field. Morris had experimented with natural dyes and fabrics required for his embroidered hangings since the earliest days of the firm, and sourced woollen serge from the

FIG. 6 Block-printing *Lodden* (designed 1884) at the Morris & Co. workshop, Merton Abbey, London, 23 March 1931.

Manchester firm Heaton & Co. The same firm probably provided *Utrecht Velvet*, a stamped wool and mohair plush that imitated velvets made in the 1600s and was suitably hardwearing for upholstery [FIG. 7].

Morris worked with other manufacturers based in the north of England as he developed his ideas for printed furnishing fabrics, initially based on naturalistic floral patterns similar to those he remembered from his childhood. He found his most sympathetic and resourceful collaborator in Thomas Wardle, a commercial dye chemist with works in Leek, Staffordshire. Together they revived the use of vegetable dyes. Morris worked among the dye vats wearing a worker's smock and clogs, his hands stained dark blue, doing what he called 'journeyman's work ... delightful work, hard for the body and easy for the mind'[11] [FIG. 8]. A series of printed furnishing fabrics in an array of colours that now define the Morris & Co. style was manufactured in Leek, including *Marigold*, *Tulip*, *Iris* and *Honeysuckle*. However, two years of productive collaboration with Wardle ended in 1877, with Morris dissatisfied by their attempts to manufacture designs for discharge printing using indigo dye (see pp.22–3). That same year, Morris relocated the showroom to 264 Oxford Street, London's main shopping thoroughfare, a move that provided more display space for the expanding ranges and proved to be more convenient for passing trade.

PATTERN DESIGN AND STRUCTURE

The floral patterns of the mid-1870s reflect Morris's lifelong love of gardens and the semi-naturalistic planting coming into fashion as part of the wider Arts and Crafts Movement. From 1871 he rented Kelmscott Manor, deep in the Oxfordshire countryside, for weekends and holidays. The house and surrounding water meadows were a vital retreat and also provided immediate sources of inspiration for many designs. It was here that Morris watched a thrush feeding on strawberries from the kitchen garden,

a moment that inspired *Strawberry Thief*, a pattern that is full of life, yet captured within the stylized, flat shapes that were the foundation of his designs. Morris aimed to suggest natural beauty with 'abundance and richness of detail' while combining 'clearness of form and firmness', also arguing for the necessity of a logical structure that looks as if 'it could not have been otherwise, which prevents the eye wearying of the repetition of the pattern'.[12]

A structure of predominantly diagonal or vertical lines of branches characterizes many informal patterns, such as *Willow Bough*, and the simple layered effect of *Marigold* or *Acanthus*, where the main motif stands out against a detailed background. Others used an all-over 'net' or diaper framework. These could vary in scale from tiny prints designed for curtain linings, such as *Flowerpot*, which unusually Morris felt was also appropriate as a dress fabric, to the very largest wallpaper repeats such as *Sunflower*. Other large-scale patterns such as *Golden Bough* and *Autumn Flowers* foreground the formal medieval-style 'ogee' structure of curved compartments with vertical half-drop repeats. Morris advocated large patterns even in small rooms: '... if properly designed they are more restful to the eye than small ones: on the whole, a pattern where the structure is large and the details much broken up is the most useful ...'.[13] Other patterns have a definite horizontal format, with symmetrical, mirrored designs,

FIG. 9 Trial sample for *Iris* printed cotton, 1876. Designed by William Morris. Block-printed cotton, Thomas Wardle, 59 × 45 cm (23¼ × 17¾ in). V&A: T.45-1919. Given by Morris & Co.

including *Honeysuckle*, which may reflect Morris's ongoing research into such 'turnover' patterns particularly suitable for setting up on a loom. This fertilization of motifs and visual structures across Morris's different preoccupations can be followed throughout his designs for embroidery, print, weaving, carpets and tapestries. To protect his designs from copyists, Morris registered them at the Patent Office, a documentation system that has enabled the dating of many products. A sample of *Iris* reveals the roll-end, stamped with the Bloomsbury address, as well as a diamond mark with a coded date [FIG. 9].

Textiles, traded between cultures and nations across the globe for centuries, often exhibit and exchange a 'visual language' of forms, materials and processes. In nineteenth-century Britain many designers, particularly those engaged in design reform such as Morris, Owen Jones (1809–1874), Christopher Dresser (1834–1904) and others, took inspiration from non-European and historical precedents. While British flowers and birds dominate Morris's patterns, the influence of the design and textiles of India, Iran and Turkey that he studied at the V&A and in private collections was profound, infusing his decisions about colour and

FIG. 10. Point paper for
Dove and Rose painted in the
Morris & Co. workshops from
Morris's original design of 1879,
18.2 × 46.5 cm (7¼ × 18⅜ in).
William Morris Gallery, London
Borough of Waltham Forest
(BLA 451)

structure and complicating the idea of his work as archetypally English. Rowan Bain, Qaisra M. Khan and others have built on existing analysis of Morris's interactions with art from the Islamic world, showing that Morris adapted motifs from Iranian metalwork and Turkish silks and ceramics from his personal collection for new designs for wallpapers and fabrics.[14] Informed by his studies, Morris understood that woven fabrics especially demanded a 'higher and more dignified style of design', and accordingly a fourteenth-century Italian silk in the V&A collection designed with paired birds may have inspired woven designs such as *Peacock and Dragon*.[15] This was one of Morris's early efforts to emulate the gravitas of historical woven textiles and, importantly, one he made himself, rather than having it contracted out to a manufacturer.

WEAVING

Woven fabrics at their most basic are formed from a simple, even mesh of crossed threads made on a frame or loom (a plain or tabby weave). Strong warp threads wound onto the horizontal beams of the loom form the length of the fabric and weft threads wound around a shuttle are fed back and forth between alternate warps to create the 'web'. Plain woven cotton or linen was usually the ground for the printed furnishing fabrics. Velvet, woven with an additional warp to create the pile, was also a base for printed Morris

designs. Woven patterning, however, is a structural part of the fabric, made with more complex weave formations often facilitated by additional warps or wefts. By varying the binding systems of the warps and wefts, and employing different types, weights and colours of warp and weft yarn from the infinite variations and combinations of fibres, a vast range of effects in woven fabrics is possible, a potential that Morris fully realized. Morris & Co. woven patterns include two- and three -ply weaves, woollen compound twills, silk and wool double cloths, silk tissues, brocades, brocatelles and damasks.[16] With the help of two experienced weavers, Morris was able to design and weave with a great understanding of the techniques and materials involved, and this underpinned both the beauty and the technical success of his fabrics.

Most of Morris's textiles were made on looms with a Jacquard attachment, an 1820s invention that mechanized complex woven designs. After completing a design at the drawing board, Morris himself, or a trusted employee, transferred each binding point of warp and weft into a coloured grid, the point paper [FIG. 10]. The point paper is used to translate the design line by line, with a simple punch machine producing a series of hole-punched cards that are threaded together to be passed through the Jacquard attachment above. The warp threads, released by the relevant card at the right moment, are automatically lifted for the weft, or wefts, being inserted by the weaver to create a line of pattern.

MERTON ABBEY WORKS

A photograph of the Morris & Co. weaving workshop shows the hand-operated Jacquard looms in use [FIG. 11]. Morris's ability to develop and execute ambitious ideas was transformed by moving production to old textile mills at Merton Abbey, ideally situated near the river Wandle, to the south of London. There he revived traditional processes for dyeing, printing and weaving on a grand scale, providing relatively well-paid work for crafts men and women. Morris was finally able to custom-build the indigo dye vats necessary for the discharge-dyeing process and he designed a series of complex patterns that exploited the full potential of the technique, including *Strawberry Thief* and *Wandle*. A 'fent', or trial sample,

illustrates the discharge method: the entire piece of fabric has been dyed in the vat, dried, then printed with two sets of blocks, one with a strong bleach to remove all the blue, and one with a weaker solution to leave a paler shade. The pattern was completed by surface-printing additional colours [FIG. 12].

From the later 1880s, with his assistant John Henry Dearle (1859–1932) increasingly taking on responsibilities and May Morris overseeing the embroidery workroom,

Morris focused on the Socialist League and other concerns, publishing poetry and, in 1890, the novel *News from Nowhere*, which envisaged a utopia with art and making at the centre of life. In 1891 he founded the Kelmscott Press, which produced medieval-style books using his designs for typefaces, bindings and illustrations, culminating in his edition of the works of Chaucer. This last was published shortly before his death in 1896, at the age of only 62.

AFTER MORRIS

An image of the shop – now named Morris & Company Decorators Ltd – from 1919 shows that *Daisy* and designs from the earliest years were essential to the firm as it adapted to changing taste into the twentieth century [FIG. 13]. Dearle was well equipped to manage artistic direction, having joined as an apprentice and worked closely with Morris on designs for his most ambitious carpets and tapestries, also designing for weave and print within the house style. Jeffrey & Co. continued to manufacture wallpapers until 1927, when the company was bought by Arthur Sanderson & Sons. After Dearle's death his son Duncan Dearle (1893–1954) oversaw Morris & Co. design and production of textiles at Merton Abbey, but in 1940 the firm entered liquidation. Arthur Sanderson & Sons acquired the company and archive

and still produces textiles and wallpapers under the Morris & Co. name.

In 2023, about 130 years after it was designed, *Yare* was selected for an enterprising range of football clothing, with sales raising funds for the Walthamstow Football Club women's team [FIG. 14]. While the mass-production methods and polyester fabric are inevitably in opposition to Arts and Crafts values, the project reflects continued interest in Morris's patterns, connecting to the local community and helping to promote awareness of his social principles. 'Home' and 'Away' *Yare* tops are now part of the V&A collection, joining other recent works that continue the story of Morris & Co. patterns at the museum, facilitating discussion of their meaning and value for artistic and practical reinterpretations in the digital age.[17] While designed by Dearle, with its symmetrical, organized composition of swirling acanthus leaves and stylized flowers, *Yare* is typical of the Morris brand. It symbolizes William Morris's inspiring vision of the potential for people to live in harmony with the environment, and of simple, beautiful things made without harm to fellow human beings or the natural world.

The selection of patterns extends beyond William Morris's death in 1896 to include later Morris & Co. designs that reveal how his influence was extended and adapted at the end of the nineteenth century and into the twentieth. It closes with the final wallpaper design issued by Morris & Co.: Kathleen Kersey's Bird and Pomegranate *(1924–?27), which was inspired by William Morris's design* Fruit, *made around 60 years earlier. For dates of fabric works, we have used Linda Parry's 2013* William Morris Textiles *as our guide, while for wallpapers, we have relied largely on Emma Hardy's PhD thesis:* A Modern but Useful Art: William Morris, Jeffrey & Co. and the Morris & Co. Wallpapers 1864–c.1928. *This establishes the likely date of first production, using as its main source the logbooks housed in the Morris Archives at Sanderson. Patterns have been organized loosely chronologically but not in traditional groupings of designs, providing an opportunity for interesting juxtapositions.*

Although we have preferred to use designs produced before 1927 in the case of wallpapers and 1940 in the case of fabrics, on occasion we have illustrated 1950s Sanderson wallpapers made from the original blocks. As the aim is to inspire rather than to offer an exhaustive guide, we have not included some of the small, partial patterns in the V&A collection. In the captions, we have included the place of manufacture, and a simple medium line for the sample illustrated. It is important to note that other mediums may also have been used.

PATTERN & DESIGN

(opposite top): E.3720-1927
(opposite bottom); Circ.141-
1959 (right)

Daisy, 1862–4. Designed
by Morris. Block-printed in
distemper on paper, Jeffrey
& Co. V&A: E.442-1919

opposite, clockwise from top left: E.450-1919; E.3701-1927; E.3700-1927; E.3702-1927

Trellis, 1862. Designed by Morris, birds by Philip Webb. Block-printed in distemper on paper, Jeffrey & Co. V&A: E.452-1919 (left);

Fruit (or *Pomegranate*), 1866.
Designed by Morris. Block-
printed in distemper on paper,
Jeffrey & Co. V&A: E.446-1919
(opposite); E.2745-1980 (right);
E.2744-1980 (p.34); E.3710-
1927 (p.35 top); E.3711-1927
(p.35 bottom)

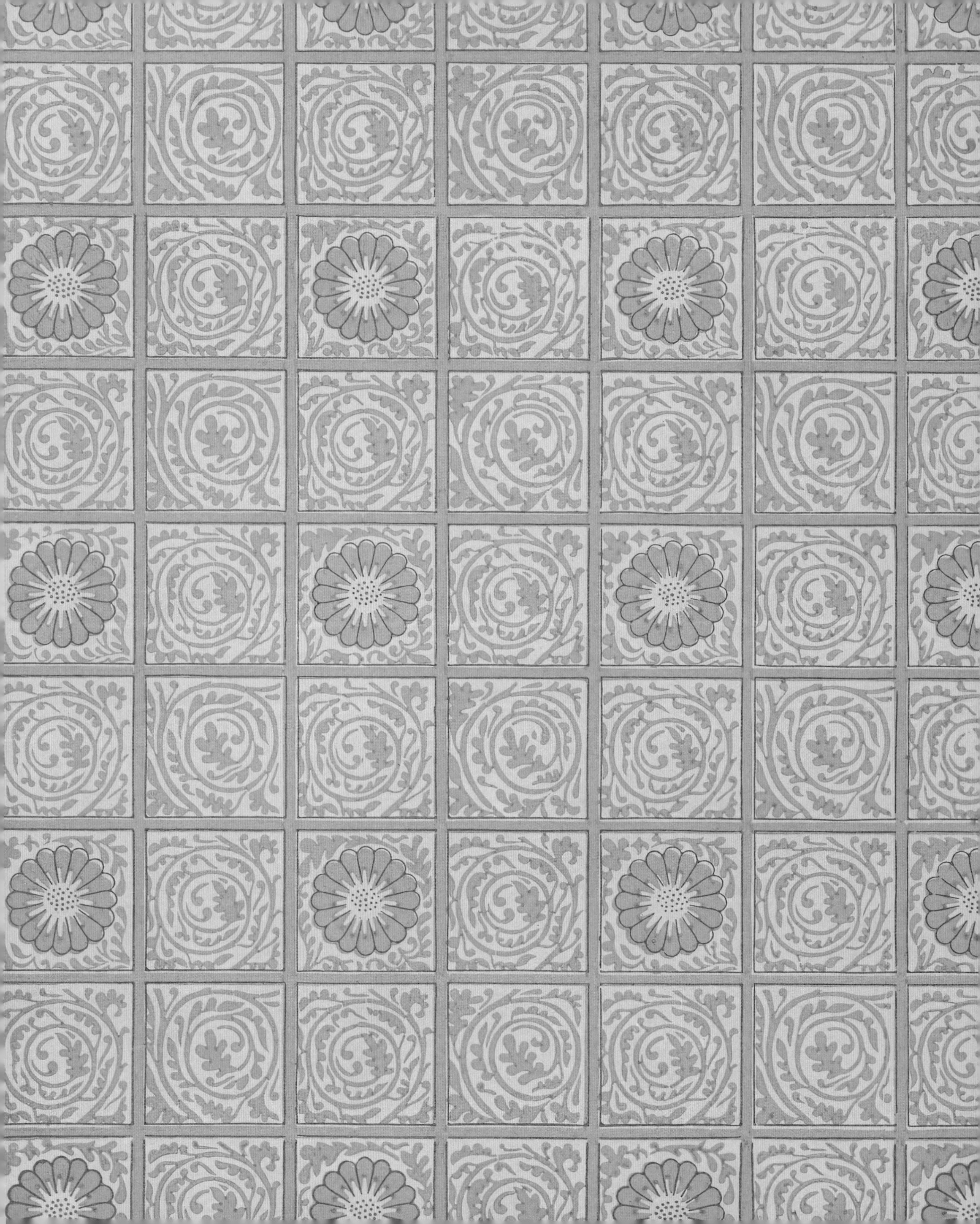

Diaper, c.1868–70. Designed by Webb. Block-printed in distemper on paper, Jeffrey & Co. V&A: E.454-1919 (opposite); E.458-1919 (right)

Indian, c.1868–70. Probably designed by George Gilbert Scott Jr for Morris & Co. Block-printed in distemper on paper, Jeffrey & Co. V&A: E.3706-1927 (left); E.3707-1927 (opposite); E.3708-1927 (p.40 top); E.757-1915 (p.40 bottom); E.3709-1927 (p.41 top); E.757-1915 (p.41 bottom)

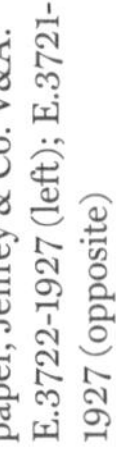

Queen Anne, c.1868–70.
Designed by Morris, possibly
from a design by G.F. Bodley
and his associates. Block-
printed in distemper on
paper, Jeffrey & Co. V&A:
E.3722-1927 (left); E.3721-
1927 (opposite)

Spray, c.1868–70. Designed by Morris, possibly from a design by G.F. Bodley and his associates. Block-printed in distemper on paper,

Jeffrey & Co. V&A: E.3713-1927 (opposite); E.3714-1927 (right top); E.2807-1927 (right bottom)

Venetian, c.1868–70.
Designed by Morris, possibly from a design by G.F. Bodley and his associates. Block-printed in distemper on paper, Jeffrey & Co.
V&A: E.3715-1927 (left top); E.3717-1927 (left bottom); E.3716-1927 (opposite)

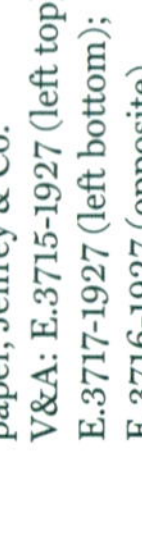

Small Stem, c.1868. Adapted
from an 1830s British design.
Block-printed cotton, Thomas
Clarkson, later Wardle & Sons.
V&A: T.37-1979 (right)

Jasmine Trellis, c.1868–70.
Designed by Morris.
Block-printed cotton, Thomas
Clarkson, later Wardle & Sons.
V&A: T.70-1953 (opposite)

Branch, c.1868–70. Designed by Morris. Block-printed in distemper on paper, Jeffrey & Co. V&A: E.3699-1927 (left)

Scroll, c.1868–70. Designed by Morris. Block-printed in distemper on paper, Jeffrey & Co. V&A: E.639-1915 (opposite top);

E.3698-1927 (opposite bottom left); Circ.279-1959 (opposite bottom right)

Jasmine, 1872. Designed by Morris. Block-printed in distemper on paper, Jeffrey & Co. V&A: E.475-1919 (opposite top); E.2753-1980 (opposite bottom left); E.476-1919 (opposite bottom right); E.2751-1980 (right)

Lily, 1874. Designed by Morris. Block-printed in distemper on paper, Jeffrey & Co. V&A: Circ.276-1959 (opposite top); E.2766-1980 (opposite bottom); E.484-1919 (right)

Tulip and Willow, 1873. Designed by Morris. Block-printed linen, Thomas Clarkson (initial trials only; from 1883 in indigo discharge, Merton Abbey). V&A: Circ.91-1933 (opposite)

Vine, 1874. Designed by Morris. Block-printed in distemper on paper, Jeffrey & Co. V&A: E.485-1919 (left top); Circ.278-1959 (left bottom)

Powdered, 1874. Designed by Morris. Block-printed in distemper on paper; Jeffrey & Co. V&A: Circ.277-1959 (opposite top); E.2759-1980 (opposite bottom); E.2761-1980 (right)

Powdered wallpaper, 1874. Block-printed cotton, Merton Abbey. V&A: T.209-1953 (opposite)

Scroll or *Little Scroll* or *Willow*, 1874/c.1895. Designed by Morris c.1895, adapted from background pattern of

Willow, 1874. Designed by Morris. Block-printed in distemper on paper, Jeffrey & Co. V&A: Circ.285-1959 (left)

Utrecht Velvet, c.1871.
Stamped mohair plush.
Probably adapted from range
produced by J. Aldam Heaton,
Manchester. Sold by Morris,
Marshall, Faulkner & Co. from
about 1871. V&A: T.210-1953
(opposite)

Acanthus, 1876. Designed
by Morris. Block-printed
velveteen, Wardle. V&A:
Circ.7A-1966 (right)

Acanthus, 1875. Designed by Morris. Block-printed in distemper on paper, Jeffrey & Co. V&A: E.494-1919 (left); E.496-1919 (opposite)

Marigold, 1875. Designed by Morris. Block-printed in distemper on paper, Jeffrey & Co. V&A: E.483-1919 (left); E.777-1915 (opposite top); Circ.275-1959 (opposite bottom)

Marigold, 1875. Designed by
Morris. Block-printed fabric,
Wardle. V&A: Circ.496-1965
(opposite top; silk); T.638-1919
(opposite bottom; cotton);
T.639-1919 (right; cotton)

Carnation, 1875. Probably designed by Kate Faulkner. Block-printed cotton, Wardle. V&A: T.591-1919 (left); T.44-1919 (opposite)

Indian Diaper, before December 1875. Designed by Morris. Block-printed cotton, Wardle. V&A: T.585-1919 (pp.72–3)

Larkspur, c.1870–72. Designed by Morris. Block-printed in distemper on paper, Jeffrey & Co. V&A: E.2218-1913

(opposite top); E.468-1919 (opposite bottom)

Larkspur, 1874. Designed by Morris from earlier wallpaper. Block-printed silk, Wardle. V&A: Circ.493-1965 (right)

Larkspur (multicolour),
1875. Designed by Morris.
Block-printed in distemper
on paper, Jeffrey & Co. V&A:
E.2771-1980 (left); E.472-
1919 (opposite)

Tulip, 1875. Designed by Morris. Block-printed cotton, Wardle. V&A: T.629-1919 (opposite); Circ.408-1953 (right); Circ.21-1954 (p.80 top); T.43-1919 (p.80 bottom); Circ.409-1953 (p.81); T.628-1919 (p.82 top); Circ.410-1953 (p.82 bottom); T.627-1919 (p.83)

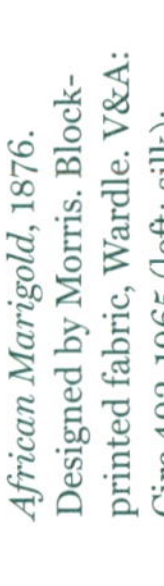

African Marigold, 1876. Designed by Morris. Block-printed fabric, Wardle. V&A: Circ.492-1965 (left; silk); Circ.42–1954 (opposite; cotton); T.641-1919 (p.86; silk); Circ.411-1953 (p.87; cotton)

Honeysuckle, 1876. Designed by Morris. Block-printed fabric, Wardle. V&A: Circ.196-1934 (left; cotton); Circ.87-1933 (opposite; cotton);

Circ.489-1965 (p.90; silk); Circ.490-1965 (p.91; silk); Circ.491-1965 (p.92; silk); Circ.487-1965 (p.93; silk)

Iris, 1876. Designed by Morris.
Block-printed cotton, Wardle.
V&A: T.141-1919 (pp.94–5)

Little Chintz, 1876. Designed by Morris. Block-printed cotton, Wardle. V&A: T:40–1919 (pp.100–1)

Crown Imperial or *Dixon of Bradford*, 1876. Designed by Morris. Woven wool and mohair by Dixon. V&A: T.22–1919 (pp.96–7)

(left top); T.157G-1986 (left bottom); T.157C-1986 (opposite top); T.157A-1986 (opposite bottom)

Samples of woven wool, 1986, closely based on *Mohair Damask* design by Morris. Made in Germany for Unika Vaev. V&A: T.157E-1986

Pimpernel, 1876. Designed by Morris. Block-printed in distemper on paper, Jeffrey & Co. V&A: E.497-1919

(opposite); E.499-1919 (right top); E.498-1919 (right bottom)

Bluebell or *Columbine*, 1876. Designed by Morris. Block-printed cotton, Wardle. V&A: Circ.44-1956 (pp.106–7)

Snakeshead, 1876. Designed by Morris. Block-printed cotton, Wardle. V&A: T.37-1919 (left); T.644-1919 (opposite top left); T.643-1919 (opposite top right); Circ.46-1956 (opposite bottom)

Tulip and Rose, 1876. Designed by Morris. 3-ply carpeting and furnishing fabric, Heckmondwike Manufacturing Company, Yorkshire.

V&A: T.110-1972 (left top); T.20-1968 (left bottom); Circ.390A-1970 (opposite)

Wreath, 1876. Designed by Morris. Block-printed in distemper on paper, Jeffrey & Co. V&A: E.501-1919 (opposite); E.500-1919 (right)

Bird, 1877–8. Designed by Morris. Woven woollen double cloth, Queen Square, later Merton Abbey. V&A: Circ.501A-1962 (pp.114–15)

Apple, 1877. Designed by Morris. Block-printed in distemper on paper, Jeffrey & Co. V&A: E.508-1919 (left); E.2217-1913 (opposite top); E.506-1919 (opposite bottom)

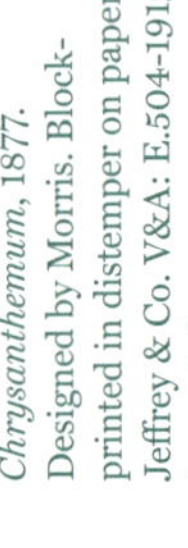

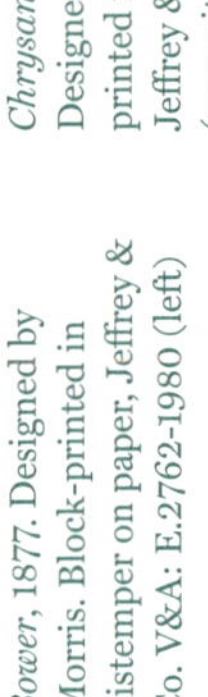

Chrysanthemum, 1877.
Designed by Morris. Block-printed in distemper on paper, Jeffrey & Co. V&A: E.504-1919 (opposite)

Bower, 1877. Designed by Morris. Block-printed in distemper on paper, Jeffrey & Co. V&A: E.2762-1980 (left)

Pomegranate, 1877. Designed by Morris. Block-printed cotton, Wardle. V&A: T.592-1919 (pp.120–1)

Peony, 1877. Designed by Kate Faulkner. Block-printed cotton, Wardle. V&A: T.587-1919 (right)

Ceiling, 1877. Designed by Morris. Block-printed in distemper on paper, Jeffrey & Co. V&A: E.510-1919 (opposite)

Rose, 1877. Designed by Morris. Block-printed in distemper on paper, Jeffrey & Co. V&A: E.503-1919 (left); E.502-1919 (opposite)

Swivel, 1877. Designed by Morris. Woven fabric. Contractors, later Merton Abbey. V&A: T.21-1968 (opposite top left; wool and silk); T.27-1919 (opposite top right; cotton and silk)

Vine and Pomegranate, c.1877. Designed by Morris or Kate Faulkner. Woven woollen triple cloth, Heckmondwike Manufacturing Company. V&A: T.23-1919 (opposite bottom); Circ.383-1962 (right)

Peacock and Dragon, 1878. Designed by Morris. Woven woollen twill, Queen Square, later Merton Abbey. V&A: T.65A-1933 (pp.126–7)

Acorn, 1879. Designed by Morris. Block-printed in distemper on paper, Jeffrey & Co. V&A: Circ.282-1959 (opposite)

Bird and Vine, 1879. Designed by Morris. Woven woollen fabric, Queen Square, later Merton Abbey. V&A: T.14-1919 (right)

Acanthus, 1879. Designed by Morris. Woven woollen damask, Queen Square, later Merton Abbey. V&A: T.28-1919 (pp.128-9)

Dove and Rose, 1879. Designed by Morris. Woven silk and wool double cloth, Alexander Morton & Co., later Merton Abbey. V&A: Circ.610-1954 (left); T.26-1919 (opposite); T.64-1919 (p.134); Circ.126-1953 (p.135)

Flower Garden, 1879. Designed by Morris. Woven silk, silk. Queen Square, later Merton Abbey. V&A: T.67-1919 (left and opposite; silk);

Circ.94-1953 (p.138; silk and wool); Circ.80A-1966 (p.139; silk and wool)

Sunflower, 1879. Designed by Morris. Block-printed in metallic paint and lacquer on embossed paper, Jeffrey & Co. V&A: E.2864-1980

(opposite); E.817-1915 (right top; block-printed in distemper on paper); E.513-1919 (right bottom; block-printed in distemper on paper)

Loop Trail, 1877. Designed by
Kate Faulkner. Block-printed
in distemper on paper, Jeffrey
& Co. V&A: E.843-1915 (left)

Bramble, 1879. Designed by
Kate Faulkner. Block-printed
in distemper on paper, Jeffrey
& Co. Reprinted Sanderson
c.1955. V&A: E.1414-1979
(opposite)

Carnation, 1880. Designed by Kate Faulkner. Machine printed in distemper on paper. V&A: E.818-1915 (opposite)

Mallow, 1879. Designed by Kate Faulkner. Block-printed in distemper on paper, Jeffrey & Co. V&A: E.811-1915 (left)

Brother Rabbit, 1881–2.
Designed by Morris. Block-
printed cotton, Merton Abbey.
V&A: T.645-1919 (right top);
T.646-1919 (right bottom);
T.647-1919 (opposite top);
T.648-1919 (opposite bottom);
T.649-1919 (pp.148–9).

Madras Muslin, 1880.
Designed by Morris. Woven
silk and cotton leno (gauze),
Alexander Morton & Co.
V&A: T.658-1919 (opposite);
T.657-1919 (right)

Poppy, 1881. Designed by Morris. Block-printed in distemper on paper, Jeffrey & Co. V&A: E.521-1919 (left; with metallic paint); E.819-1915 (opposite)

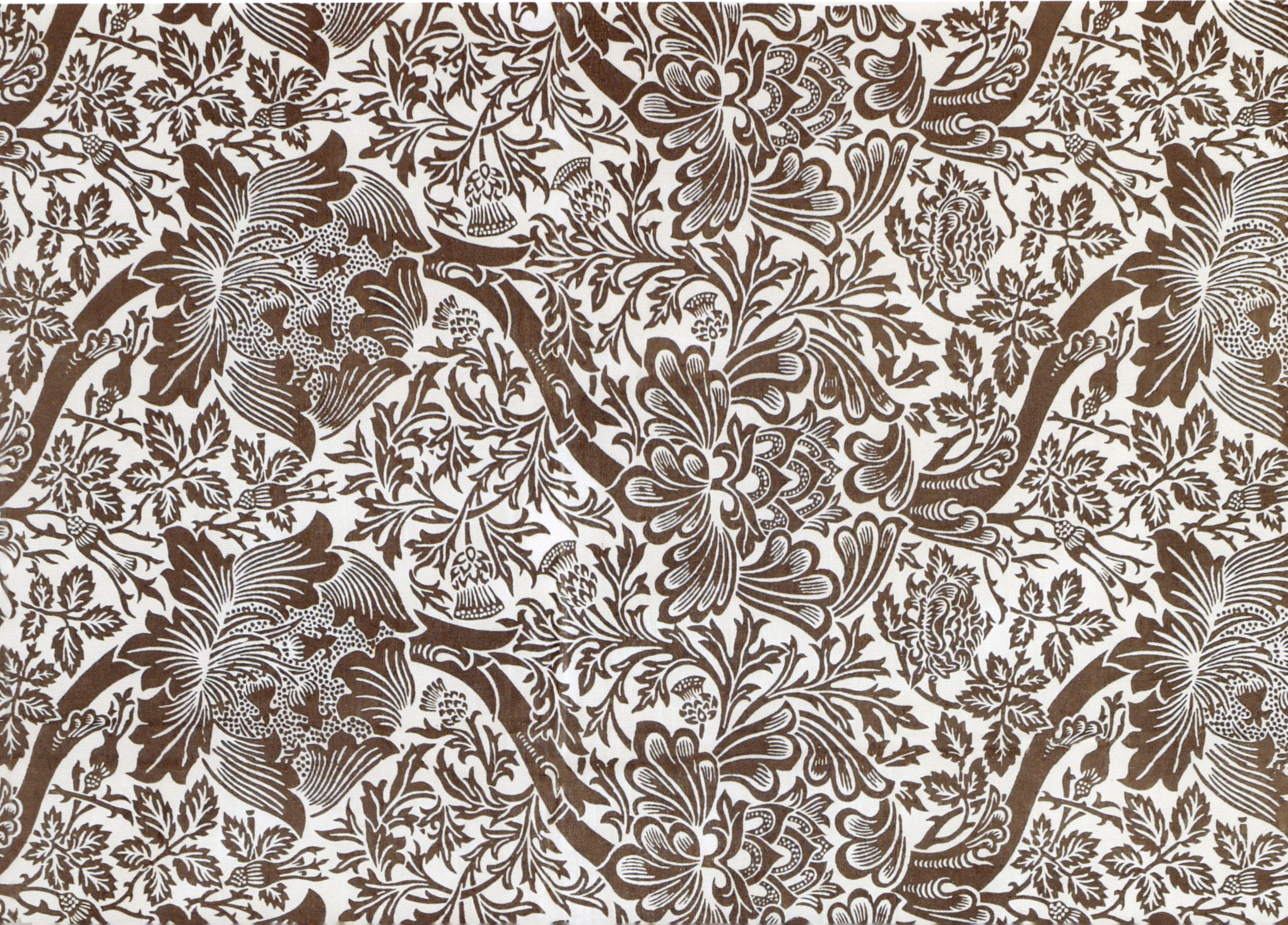

Rose and Thistle, before April 1881. Designed by Morris. Block-printed cotton, Merton Abbey. V&A: T.634-1919 (opposite top); T.637-1919 (opposite bottom); T.33-1919 (right); Circ.416-1953 (p.156 top); T.32-1919 (p.156 bottom); Circ.83-1953 (p.157 top); T.635-1919 (p.157 bottom)

Bird and Anemone, 1881–2. Designed by Morris. Block-printed cotton, Merton Abbey. V&A: T.650-1919 (opposite top); T.654-1919 (opposite bottom); T.653-1919 (right); T.651-1919 (p.160 top); T.652-1919 (p.160 bottom); T.655-1919 (p.162 top); T.656-1919 (p.162 bottom)

Bird and Anemone, 1882.
Designed by Morris. Block-
printed in distemper on paper,
Jeffrey & Co. V&A: E.530-1919
(opposite)

Oak, 1881. Designed by Morris. Woven silk damask, J.O. Nicholson, later Merton Abbey. V&A: T.74-1919 (right); T.52-1946 (p.164 top); Circ.86-1957 (p.164 bottom; rayon damask; reproduction by Courtaulds Textiles for Sanderson *c*.1945–55); Circ.124-1953 (p.165)

St James, 1881. Designed by Morris. Woven silk damask and figured silk, J.O. Nicholson, later Merton Abbey. V&A: Circ.438-1953 (pp.166–7)

St James, 1881. Designed by Morris. Block-printed in distemper on paper, Jeffrey & Co. V&A: E.528-1919 (opposite; with metallic paint); E.2862-1980 (right)

St James's Ceiling, 1881. Designed by Morris. Block-printed in distemper on paper, Jeffrey & Co. V&A: E.594–1919 (pp.170–1)

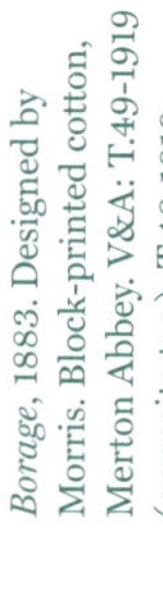

Borage, 1883. Designed by
Morris. Block-printed cotton,
Merton Abbey. V&A: T.49-1919
(opposite top); T.48-1919
(opposite bottom)

Wreathnet, 1882. Designed by
Morris. Block-printed cotton,
Merton Abbey. V&A: T.50-
1919 (left)

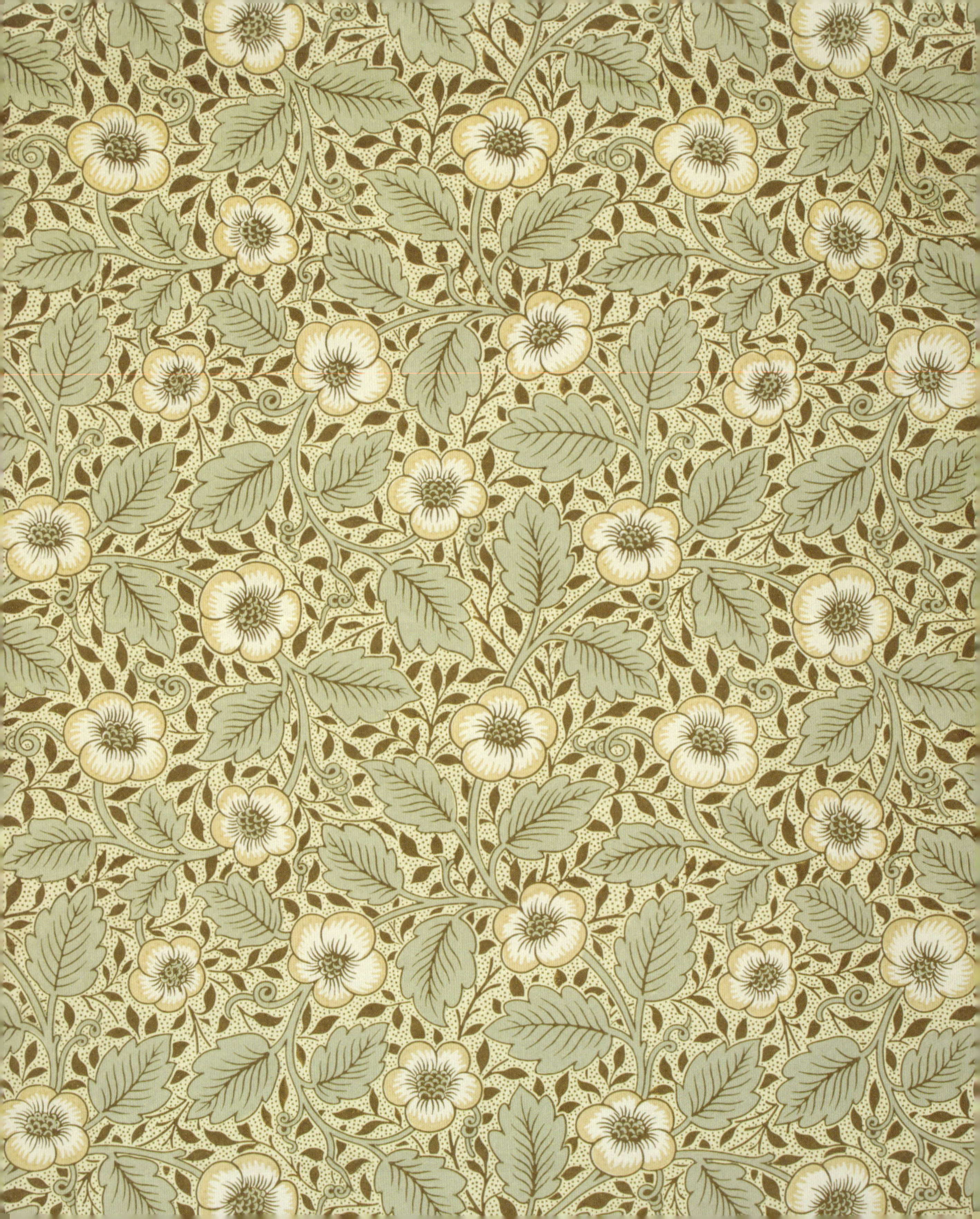

Christchurch, 1883. Designed by Morris. Block-printed in distemper on paper, Jeffrey & Co. V&A: E.2758-1980 (opposite)

Grafton, 1883. Designed by Morris. Block-printed in distemper on paper, Jeffrey & Co. V&A: E.533-1919 (right)

Campion, 1883. Designed by Morris. Woven wool, Merton Abbey and Heckmondwike Manufacturing Company Ltd. V&A: Circ.385-1962 (pp.176–7)

Corncockle, 1883. Designed by Morris. Block-printed cotton, Merton Abbey. V&A: Circ.87-1953 (left); Circ.84-1953 (opposite); T.590-1919 (p.180); T.168-1973 (p.181)

Eyebright, 1883. Designed by Morris. Block-printed cotton, Merton Abbey. V&A: T.51–1912 (opposite)

Evenlode, 1883. Designed by Morris. Block-printed cotton, Merton Abbey. V&A: T.46–1912 (left)

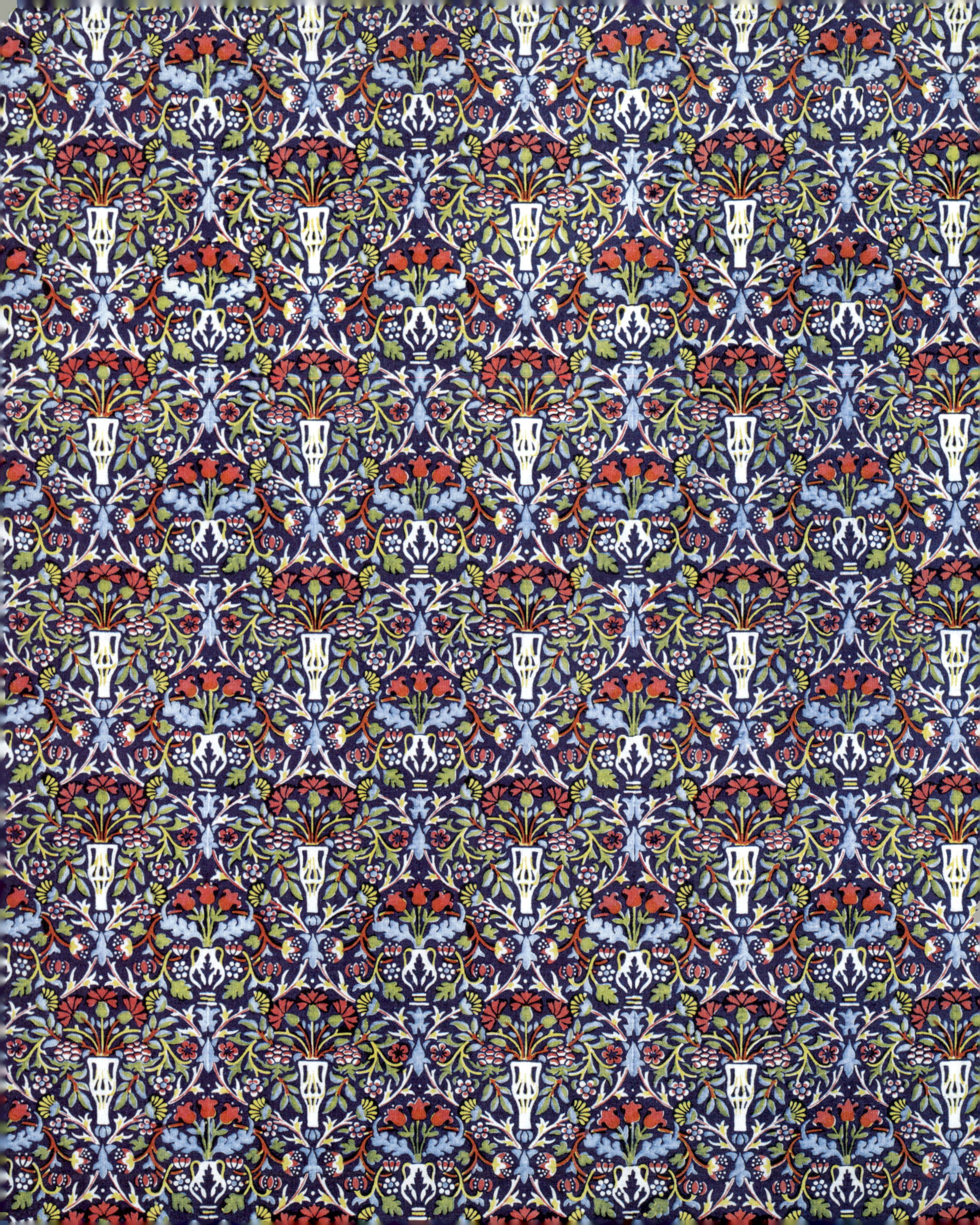

Flowerpot, 1883. Designed by Morris. Block-printed cotton, Merton Abbey. V&A: T.51–1919 (opposite)

Kennet, 1883. Designed by Morris. Block-printed cotton, velveteen and woven fabric. Printed Merton Abbey. V&A: T.604-919 (right; velveteen and silk); T.69-1919 (p.186 top; woven silk and linen); T.606-1919 (p.186 bottom; block-printed cotton); T.50-1946 (p.187; woven silk)

Honeysuckle, 1883. Designed by May Morris. Block-printed in distemper on paper, Jeffrey & Co. V&A: Circ.9-1954 (opposite); V&A: E.668-1915 (right)

Rose, 1883. Designed by Morris. Block-printed cotton and linen, Merton Abbey. V&A: T.53-1912 (pp.190–1)

Strawberry Thief, 1883.
Designed by Morris. Block-
printed cotton, Merton Abbey.
V&A: Circ.90-1933 (pp.192–3)

Violet and Columbine, 1883.
Designed by Morris. Woven
wool and mohair fabric,
Merton Abbey. V&A: T.11-1919
(opposite); T.674D-1974 (right)

Wey, c.1883. Designed by Morris. Block-printed fabric, Merton Abbey. V&A: T.603-1919 (left top; cotton); T.602-1919 (left bottom; cotton); T.601-1919 (opposite); T.87a-1980 (p.198; velveteen)

Granada, 1884. Designed by Morris. Woven silk velvet brocaded with gilt thread, Merton Abbey. V&A: T.4-1919 (right)

Windrush, 1883. Designed by Morris. Block-printed cotton and linen, Merton Abbey. V&A T.617-1919 (p.200–1; cotton); Circ.424-1953 (p.202; cotton); T.618-1919 (p.203; linen)

Cray, 1884. Designed by
Morris. Block-printed cotton,
Merton Abbey. V&A: T.34-1919
(opposite top); Circ.82-1953
(opposite bottom); T.607-1919
(right)

T.518:11-1996 (p.209 top and bottom; printed cotton reissued in new colourways by Harris Fabrics Ltd, 1995)

Wandle, 1884. Designed by Morris. Block-printed cotton, Merton Abbey. V&A: T.425-1934 (opposite); T.594-1919 (p.208); T.518:2-1996 and

Lodden, 1884. Designed by Morris. Block-printed cotton, Merton Abbey. V&A: T.39-1919 (left)

Blossom, 1885. Designed by Kate Faulkner. Block-printed in distemper on paper. V&A: E.2767-1980 (pp.212–13)

Wild Tulip, 1884. Designed by Morris. Block-printed in distemper on paper, Jeffrey & Co. V&A: E.536-1919 (left; with metallic paint); E.538-1919 (opposite)

Ceiling, 1884. Designed by Morris. Block-printed in distemper on paper, Jeffrey & Co. V&A: Circ.288-1959 (opposite)

Fritillary, 1885. Designed by Morris. Block-printed in distemper on paper, Jeffrey & Co. V&A: E.545-1919 (right); E.543-1919 (p.216); Circ.283-1959 (p.217)

Garden Tulip, 1885. Designed by Morris. Block-printed in distemper on paper, Jeffrey & Co. V&A: E.551-1919 (opposite top); E.552-1919 (opposite bottom); E.550-1919 (right)

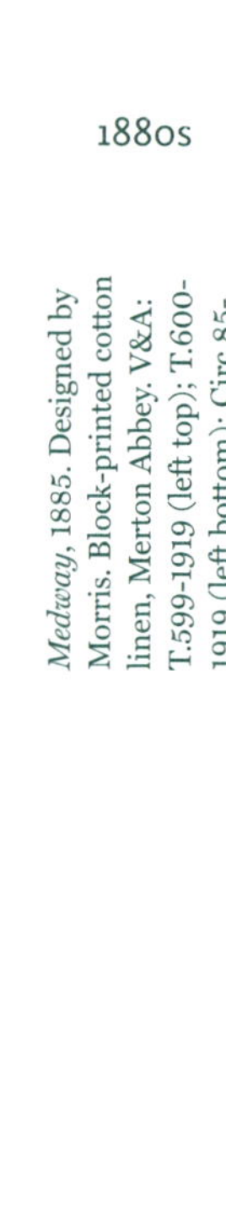

Medway, 1885. Designed by Morris. Block-printed cotton linen, Merton Abbey. V&A: T.599-1919 (left top); T.600-1919 (left bottom); Circ.85-1933 (opposite)

Lea, 1885. Designed by Morris. Block-printed cotton, Merton Abbey. V&A: T.609-1919 (left); T.608-1919 (opposite); T.610-1919 (p.224); T.55-1912 (p.225)

Horn Poppy, 1885. Designed by May Morris. Block-printed in distemper on paper, Jeffrey & Co. V&A: E.707-1915 (left)

Arcadia, c.1886. Designed by Mary (May) Morris. Block-printed in distemper on paper, Jeffrey & Co. V&A: E.555-1919 (opposite)

Lily and Pomegranate, 1886.
Designed by Morris. Block-
printed in distemper on paper,
Jeffrey & Co. V&A: E.2224–
1913 (opposite); E.554-1919
(right top); E.2225-1913
(right bottom)

Cherwell, 1887. Designed by Dearle. Block-printed cotton and velveteen, Merton Abbey. V&A: T.62-1946; cotton velveteen (left)

Iris, 1887–8. Designed by Dearle. Block-printed in distemper on paper, Jeffrey & Co. V&A: E.642-1915 (opposite top); E.699-1915 (opposite bottom)

Avon, c.1888. Designed by Morris and/or Dearle. Block-printed cotton, Merton Abbey. V&A: T.598-1919 (right top); T.597-1919 (right bottom)

Willow Bough[s], 1887. Designed by Morris. Block-printed in distemper on paper, Jeffrey & Co. V&A: E.557-1919 (opposite top); E.558-1919 (opposite bottom)

Borage (ceiling), 1888–90. Designed by Morris. Block-printed in distemper on paper, Jeffrey & Co. V&A: E.569-1919 (opposite bottom)

(opposite top left); E.2215-1913 (opposite top right)

Autumn Flowers, 1888–90. Designed by Morris. Block-printed in distemper on paper, Jeffrey & Co. V&A: E.2775-1980 (left); E.2214-1913

Brocatel, c.1888. Designed by Morris. Woven silk and woollen fabric, Merton Abbey. V&A: Circ.86-1953 (opposite); T.61-1946 (right)

Bruges, 1888. Designed by Morris. Block-printed in distemper on paper. V&A: E.561-1919 (left; with mica); Circ.287-1959 (opposite)

Golden Bough, c.1888. Designed by Morris. Woven silk and linen fabric, Merton Abbey. V&A: T.496-1934 (opposite)

Ispahan, c.1888. Designed by Morris. Woven woollen fabric, Merton Abbey. V&A: T.111-1953 (right)

Merton, 1888. Designed by Kate Faulkner. Machine-printed in distemper on paper, Jeffrey & Co. V&A: E.647-1915 (left)

Trent, 1888. Designed by Morris and/or Dearle. Block-printed linen, Merton Abbey. V&A: T.622-1919 (opposite);
T.620-1919 (p.244 top);
T.621-1919 (p.244 bottom);
T.55-1919 (p.245)

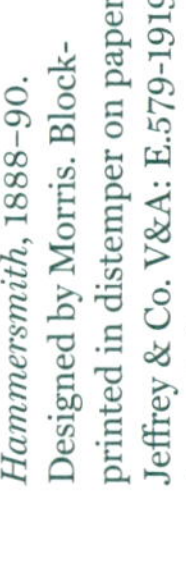

Norwich, 1888–90. Designed by Morris. Block-printed in distemper on paper, Jeffrey & Co. V&A: E.574-1919 (left top; with metallic paint); E.572-1919 (left bottom)

Hammersmith, 1888–90. Designed by Morris. Block-printed in distemper on paper, Jeffrey & Co. V&A: E.579-1919 (opposite)

Tulip and Net, 1888–9. Designed by Morris and/or Dearle. Woven wool, Merton Abbey. V&A: T.57-1934 (pp.246–7)

Double Bough[s], 1890/91.
Designed by Morris and/
or Dearle. Block-printed in
distemper on paper, Jeffrey
& Co. V&A: E.2221-1913

(opposite top); E.683-1915
(opposite bottom); E.2755-
1980 (right)

Pink and Rose (multicolour), 1893. Designed by Morris. Block-printed in distemper on paper, Jeffrey & Co. V&A: E.708-1915 (opposite)

Pink and Rose, 1888–90. Designed by Morris. Block-printed in distemper on paper, Jeffrey & Co. V&A: E.580-1919 (left)

Sunflower, c.1890. Designed by Dearle. Woven woollen fabric, Merton Abbey. V&A: T.93-1985 (right)

Persian Brocatel, c.1890. Designed by Dearle. Woven silk and wool, Merton Abbey. V&A: T.68-1919 (opposite bottom)

Helena, c.1890. Designed by Dearle. Woven silk and wool double cloth, Alexander Morton & Co. V&A: T.60-1946 (opposite top)

Wallflower, 1888–90. Designed by Morris. Block-printed in distemper on paper, Jeffrey & Co. V&A: E.575-1919 (left); E.671-1915 (opposite top); E.672-1915 (opposite bottom left); E.673-1915 (opposite bottom right)

Daffodil, c.1891. Designed by Dearle. Block-printed cotton, Merton Abbey. V&A: T.623-1919 (opposite top); T.624-1919 (opposite bottom); Circ.287-1955 (right top); Circ.431-1953 (right bottom)

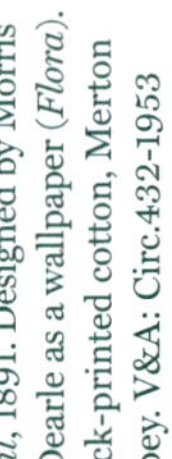

Flora, 1891. Designed by Morris or Dearle. Block-printed in distemper on paper, Jeffrey & Co. V&A: E.593-1919 (left top); E.2764-1980 (left bottom)

Trail, 1891. Designed by Morris or Dearle as a wallpaper (*Flora*). Block-printed cotton, Merton Abbey. V&A: Circ.432-1953 (opposite)

Triple Net, 1891. Designed by Morris. Block-printed in distemper on paper, Jeffrey & Co. V&A: E.689-1915 (left)

Bachelor's Button, 1892–3. Designed by Morris or Dearle. Block-printed in distemper on paper, Jeffrey & Co. V&A E.2219-1913 (opposite); E.597-1919 (p.264)

Blackthorn, 1892. Designed by Dearle. Block-printed in distemper on paper, Jeffrey & Co. V&A: E.602-1919 (right)

Apple, 1895–1900. Designed by Dearle. Woven linen and silk fabric, Merton Abbey. V&A: T.497-1934 (opposite)

Diagonal Trail, c.1893. Designed by Dearle. Woven woollen fabric, Merton Abbey. V&A: T.18-1919 (left)

Cross Twigs, c.1893. Designed by Dearle. Woven silk and linen fabric, Merton Abbey. V&A: T.58-1946 (opposite); sample weaving T.20-1919 (right)

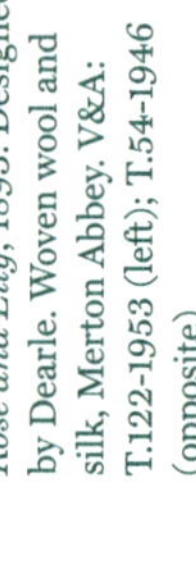

Rose and Lily, 1893. Designed by Dearle. Woven wool and silk, Merton Abbey. V&A: T.122-1953 (left); T.54-1946 (opposite)

Woodland Weeds, 1894. Designed by Dearle. Block-printed in distemper on paper, Jeffrey & Co. V&A: E.712-1915 (opposite top)

Spring Thicket, 1894. Designed by Morris. Block-printed in distemper on paper, Jeffrey & Co. V&A: E.605-1919 (opposite bottom)

Single Stem, 1894. Designed by Dearle. Block-printed in distemper on paper, Jeffrey & Co. V&A: E.2827-1980 (right)

Lechlade, 1893. Designed by Morris. Block-printed in distemper colours on paper. V&A: E.704-1915 (opposite)

Net Ceiling, 1895. Designed by Morris. Block-printed in distemper on paper, Jeffrey & Co. V&A: E.723-1915 (right)

Compton, 1895. Designed by Dearle. Block-printed in distemper on paper, Jeffrey & Co. V&A: E.606-1919 (opposite); E.607-1919 (right)

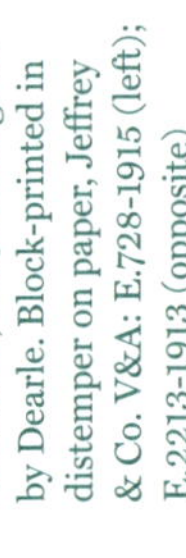

Celandine, c.1896. Designed by Dearle. Block-printed in distemper on paper, Jeffrey & Co. V&A: E.728-1915 (left); E.2213-1913 (opposite)

Fabrics Ltd after William
Morris design, 1995)

McAlpin after William Morris
design for Warner and Sons,
c.1955); T.515:1-1996 and
T.515:2-1996 (left bottom and
opposite; printed by Harris

Compton, 1896. Designed by
Dearle. Block-printed cotton
(from wallpaper blocks),
Merton Abbey. V&A: T.2-1978
(left top; printed by Stead

Granville, 1896. Designed
by Dearle. Block-printed in
distemper on paper, Jeffrey
& Co. V&A: E.724-1915
(opposite); E.725-1915 (right)

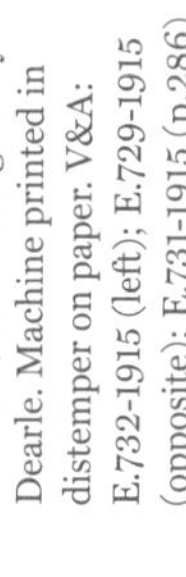

Oak Tree, 1896. Designed by
Dearle. Machine printed in
distemper on paper. V&A:
E.732-1915 (left); E.729-1915
(opposite); E.731-1915 (p.286)

Tom Tit, c.1896–7. Designed by Dearle. Machine printed in distemper on paper. V&A: E.740-1915 (right top); E.742-1915 (right bottom); E.741-1915 (p.288 top); E.739-1915 (p.288 bottom)

Thistle, 1897. Designed by Dearle. Machine printed in distemper on paper. Opposite, clockwise from top left: V&A: E.747-1915; E.745-1915; E.1432-1979 (reprinted Sanderson c.1955); E.744-1915

Anemone, 1897. Designed by Dearle. Machine printed in distemper on paper, Jeffrey & Co. V&A: E.734-1915 (opposite top left); E.2209-1913 (opposite top right); E.736-1915 (opposite bottom)

Artichoke, 1897. Designed by Dearle. Block-printed in distemper on paper, Jeffrey & Co. V&A: E.2830-1980 (right)

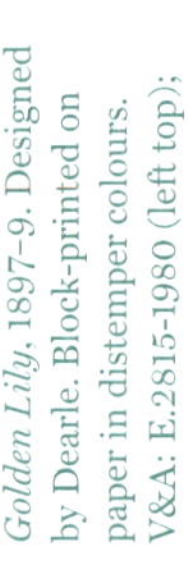

Golden Lily, 1897–9. Designed by Dearle. Block-printed on paper in distemper colours. V&A: E.2815-1980 (left top); E.2816-1980 (opposite); E.2817-1980 (left bottom)

Orchard, 1899. Designed by Dearle. Block-printed in distemper on paper, Jeffrey & Co. V&A: E.2768-1980 (opposite)

Myrtle, 1899. Designed by Morris after 1875 embroidery design. Block-printed in distemper on paper, Jeffrey & Co. V&A: Circ.27-1954 (right)

Colne, c.1899. Designer unknown, possibly Dearle for wallpaper (although printed with wallpaper blocks, no evidence of wallpaper has been found). Block-printed cotton, possibly Wardle. V&A: T.595-1919 (pp.296–7)

Garden, 1897–9. Designed by Dearle. Block-printed in distemper on paper. V&A: E.2805-1980 (opposite top left)

Foliage, 1897–9. Designed Dearle. Block-printed in distemper colours on paper, Jeffrey & Co. V&A: E.2796-1980 (opposite top right)

Meadow Sweet, 1904. Designed by Dearle. Block-printed in distemper on paper, Jeffrey & Co. V&A: E.2812-1980 (opposite bottom left)

Blackberry, 1903. Designed by Dearle. Block-printed in distemper on paper, Jeffrey & Co. V&A: E.2794-1980 (opposite bottom right)

Seaweed, 1901. Designed by Dearle. Block-printed in distemper on paper, Jeffrey & Co. V&A: E.2756-1980 (right)

Tulip Frieze, 1903. Unknown designer for Morris & Co. Block-printed in distemper on paper, Jeffrey & Co. Reprinted Sanderson c.1955. V&A: E.1422–1979 (opposite bottom)

Planet, 1901. Designed by Dearle. Block-printed in distemper on paper, Jeffrey & Co. V&A: E.2757–1980 (opposite top right)

Sprig, 1901. Unknown designer for Morris & Co. Block-printed in distemper on paper, Jeffrey & Co. Reprinted Sanderson c.1955. V&A: E.1428–1979 (opposite top left)

Daffodil, 1903. Designed by Dearle. Block-printed in distemper on paper, Jeffrey & Co. V&A: E.2792–1980 (left)

Clover, 1903. Designed by Dearle. Block-printed in distemper on paper, Jeffrey & Co. V&A: E.2778-1980 (opposite); E.2779-1980 (right)

Eden, c.1905. Designed by Dearle. Block-printed cotton, Merton Abbey, later Wardle. V&A: T.24-1955 (opposite top); Circ.288-1955 (opposite bottom)

Persian, 1904. Designed by Dearle. Block-printed in distemper on paper, Jeffrey & Co. V&A: E.2837-1980 (left)

Sweet Pea, 1908. Designed by Dearle. Block-printed in distemper on paper, Jeffrey & Co. V&A: Circ.251-1964 (opposite)

Briar, c.1906. Designed by Dearle. Block-printed cotton, Merton Abbey. V&A: T.12-1954 (left)

Musgrove or *Gothic*, before 1910. Adapted by Morris & Co. from a historical design. Woven wool, Merton Abbey. V&A: T.19-1968 (opposite)

Stripe Twill, c.1906. Designer unknown, possibly Dearle. Block-printed cotton, Merton Abbey. V&A: T.186-1982 (right top)

Acorn, before 1912. Adapted by Morris & Co. from a historical design. Embossed or stamped silk velvet, manufactured either outside the UK or by Lister's of Halifax. V&A: Circ.446–1953 (right bottom)

Harebell, 1911. Designed by Dearle. Block-printed in distemper on paper, Jeffrey & Co. Reprinted Sanderson c.1955. V&A: E.1420-1979 (opposite bottom)

Hyacinth, 1911. Designed by Dearle. Block-printed in distemper on paper, Jeffrey & Co. Reprinted Sanderson c.1955. V&A: E.1416-1979 (opposite top)

Flowering Scroll, 1908. Designed by Dearle. Block-printed in distemper on paper, Jeffrey & Co. Reprinted Sanderson c.1955. V&A: E.1431-1979 (left)

Leicester, 1911–12. Designed by Dearle. Block-printed in distemper on paper, Jeffrey & Co. Reprinted Sanderson c.1955. V&A: E.1404-1979 (p.314)

Brocade, 1911. Block-printed in distemper on paper, Jeffrey & Co. Reprinted Sanderson c.1955. V&A: E.1425-1979 (right)

Sistine, before 1912. Probably adapted by Dearle from a historical design. Woven silk and wool. V&A: T.311-1975 (opposite)

Bird and Pomegranate, 1924–7. Designed by Kathleen Kersey. Block-printed in distemper on paper, Jeffrey & Co. Reprinted Sanderson c.1955. V&A: E.1426-1979 (pp.316–17)

Arbutus, 1913. Designed by Kathleen Kersey. Block-printed in distemper on paper, Jeffrey & Co. Reprinted Sanderson c.1955. V&A: E.1413-1979 (opposite bottom right)

Brentwood, 1913. Designed by Dearle. Block-printed in distemper on paper, Jeffrey & Co. Reprinted Sanderson c.1955. V&A: E.1417-1979 (opposite bottom left)

Sweet Briar, 1911–12. Designed by Dearle. Block-printed in distemper on paper, Jeffrey & Co. Reprinted Sanderson c.1955. V&A: E.1405-1979 (opposite top right)

Michaelmas Daisy, 1912. Designed by Dearle. Block-printed in distemper on paper, Jeffrey & Co. Reprinted Sanderson c.1955. V&A: E.1403-1979 (opposite top left)

MACHINE-WOVEN CARPETS

Artichoke, 1875–80. Designed by Morris. Three-ply woollen Kidderminster-type carpet, Heckmondwike Manufacturing Company Ltd. V&A: T.188-1984 (right)

Daisy or *Grass*, 1870–5. Designed by Morris. Three-ply woollen Kidderminster-type carpet, Heckmondwike Manufacturing Company Ltd. V&A: Circ.39-1954 (opposite)

Lily, 1870s. Designed by
Morris. Machine-woven
Wilton-type carpet, woollen
pile on jute, manufactured by
Yates & Co, Wilton, Wiltshire.

V&A: Circ.65&A-1959 (left);
Circ.526-1953 (opposite
top); Circ.658-1959 (opposite
bottom); Circ.65-1959
(pp.322–3)

1   'Making the Best of it', lecture published 1881, quoted in Bain 2019, p.20

2   "The Lesser Arts of Life', 1882, in Poulson 1996, p.158

3   'The Lesser Arts of Life', 1882, quoted in Poulson 1996, p.83

4   Parry 2013, p.11

5   Letter to Cormell Price, quoted in Wild 2018, p.16, who quotes from MacCarthy 1994, p.95

6   British Library Add. MS. 45341 ff.91–110. Jane Morris, letter to May Morris, quoted in Wild 2018, p.174

7   See Hardy 2024, p.63

8   Bain 2024, pp.94–5; Hardy 2024, pp.167–9

9   Hoskins, 'Wallpaper', in Mason 2021, p.256; Hardy 2024, p.122

10 Hardy 2024, p.96

11 William Morris to Georgiana Burne-Jones 1877, quoted in Parry, 'Textiles', in Mason 2021, p.272

12 Morris, 'Textiles', in *Arts & Crafts Exhibition Society* 1888, p.28

13 Morris, 'Textiles', in *Arts & Crafts Exhibition Society* 1888, p.28

14 Bain 2024, pp.126–37

15 Some Hints on Pattern Designing', 1881, quoted in Parry 2013, p.68. V&A: 7083-1860

16 Parry 2013, p.70

17 V&A: T.86-2023 and T.87-2023

Rowan Bain, *William Morris's Flowers* (London 2019)

Rowan Bain (ed.), *Tulips and Peacocks: William Morris and Art from the Islamic World* (London and New Haven 2024)

Emma Hardy, *A Modern but Useful Art: William Morris, Jeffrey and Co. and the Morris & Co. Wallpapers 1864–c.1928*, PhD thesis, The Open University, 2024

Lesley Hoskins, 'Wallpaper', in Anna Mason (ed.), *William Morris* (London 2021), pp.237–65

Fiona MacCarthy, *William Morris: A Life for Our Time* (London 1994)

Barbara Morris, *Inspiration for Design: The Influence of the Victoria and Albert Museum* (London 1986)

William Morris, 'Textiles', in *Arts & Crafts Exhibition Society: catalogue of the first exhibition* (London 1888), pp.17–29

Linda Parry, 'Textiles', in Anna Mason (ed.), *William Morris* (London 2021), pp.267–343

Linda Parry, *William Morris Textiles*, revised edition (London 2013)

Christine Poulson (ed.), *William Morris on Art & Design* (Sheffield 1996)

Mary Schoeser, *The Art of Wallpaper: Morris & Co. in Context* (Suffolk and New York 2022)

Tessa Wild, *William Morris and His Palace of Art* (London 2018)

PICTURE CREDITS

All photos © V&A, with the following exceptions:
p.9, fig. 1 Photo: Tate
p.11, fig. 2 © The Society of Antiquaries
of London (Kelmscott Manor)
p.12, fig. 3 Photo: William Morris Gallery,
London Borough of Waltham Forest
p.15, fig. 5 © The Society of Antiquaries
of London (Kelmscott Manor)
p.16, fig. 6 Photo by Fox Photos/Hulton Archive/
Getty Images
p.20, fig. 10 Photo: William Morris Gallery,
London Borough of Waltham Forest
p.24, fig. 13 Photo: William Morris Gallery,
London Borough of Waltham Forest
p.24, fig. 14 Photo: Jake Green for Works in Public.
Courtesy Wood Street Walls

ACKNOWLEDGMENTS

For generous advice when researching for the introduction of this book, and for their thoughtful responses on the dating of wallpapers, the V&A would like to thank Dr Emma Hardy, Dr Keren Protheroe and Mary Schoeser. Any information on textiles is heavily reliant on the foundational work of Linda Parry, who died in 2023, as the current publication was conceived.

We are grateful for the guidance of many colleagues at the V&A. Foremost of these was prints curator Alice Clanachan, who helped us to find, photograph and hone details about the wallpapers. Jenny Lister was also supported by colleagues in the Performance, Furniture, and Textiles and Fashion departments, including Christopher Wilk, Oriole Cullen and Silvija Banić. The Photo Studio were very flexible at short notice, and we would especially like to thank Sarah Duncan.

Tom Windross and Susannah Priede at V&A Publishing first had the idea of how lovely it would be to bring together so many of Morris's repeating textile and wallpaper patterns in one place, while Development Editor Rebecca Fortey and Picture Researcher Amy Lewis made it possible in record time. The striking layout was conceived by Thames & Hudson's Julian Honer alongside Peter Dawson and Ronja Rønning at Grade, with Julie Hrischeva, Kirsty Seymour-Ure and Julie Bosser ably supporting the different stages of editorial and production.

INDEX OF NAMES

Jacket: *Honeysuckle*, 1876. Designed by William Morris. Block-printed silk, Wardle.
  V&A: Circ.491-1965
Cover: *Willow Bough*, 1887. Designed by William Morris. Block-printed in distemper
  on paper, Jeffrey & Co. V&A: E.558-1919
p.2: *Trent* (see p.245)
p.4: *Trellis* (see p.31)
p.26; left to right, top to bottom: *Jasmine* (see p.52), *Lily and Pomegranate* (see p.228),
  Bramble (see p.143), *Vine* (see p.56), *Loop Trail* (see p.142), *Acanthus* (see p.65),
  Bird and Anemone (see p.158), *Honeysuckle* (see p.88), *Queen Anne* (see p.42)

First published in the United Kingdom in 2025 by Thames & Hudson Ltd,
6–24 Britannia Street, London WC1X 9JD in association with the
Victoria and Albert Museum, London

First published in the United States of America in 2025 by
Thames & Hudson Inc., 500 Fifth Avenue, New York, New York 10110

William Morris: Pattern & Design © 2025 Victoria and Albert Museum,
London/Thames & Hudson Ltd, London

Text and V&A photographs © 2025 Victoria and Albert Museum, London
Design © 2025 Thames & Hudson Ltd, London

Designed by Peter Dawson, with Ronja Rønning, www.gradedesign.com

EU Authorized Representative: Interart S.A.R.L.
19 rue Charles Auray, 93500 Pantin, Paris, France
productsafety@thameshudson.co.uk
interart.fr

A CIP catalogue record for this book is available from the British Library

Library of Congress Control Number 2025935003

ISBN 978-0-500-48116-5
01

Printed and bound in China by C&C Offset Printing Co. Ltd

V&\ Publishing

The power of creativity

Discover more at vam.ac.uk